an infatuation

Stories of the
Paranormal

by Jenny Randalls
Illustrations by Philip Norman

M·Q·P

CONTENTS

The paranormal. Say that word and you can almost hear the theme tune from the *X-Files* playing in your head. It's a subject that may come to haunt you. All day long you will be asking yourself those questions that make life weird and wonderful. Is the man next door really an alien? Did your granny's cat spontaneously combust? And what about that crop circle at the back of the pub? Strange phenomena are all around you. It's difficult *not* to notice them.

When the lights are low, the log fire crackles, the conversation turns easily to those mysteries of life. It's not hard to extract dark secrets from those you thought you knew well. Everybody has a tale to tell.

'*I think I saw a ghost once.*'

'*There was a strange light that buzzed our car when we were coming home across the moors.*'

'*Next door's budgie always chirps when someone in the street is about to have an accident.*'

Unexplained experiences tumble from people's lips faster than you can say 'twilight zone'. And we all love to be terrified by odd happenings caused by unknown forces.

Over the coming pages we will look in more detail at four areas of extraordinary phenomena. We call them mysteries of time, the earth, space and the mind.

7

Mysteries of Time

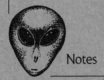

Notes

PAST LIVES

Have we ever lived before? This seems a very silly question, because we all know that people are born and they die. But can we accept the possibility of survival *after* death and the resulting immortality of the soul? If we live forever, presumably that means we have *always* lived forever. In other words, that we had many previous existences before we were born.

In fact, the idea of reincarnation is one of the most widely accepted beliefs in the world. Almost every major religion incorporates it in some way. It was even originally a part of Christianity and was only abandoned long after Christ's death.

Those who believe that our soul inhabits different bodies often talk about the law of 'karma'. This is explained in the Bible with the words 'as ye sow, so shall ye reap'. If we do evil to some person in one life we will ultimately have to pay by having the evil done to us in some future incarnation.

If a child is born with a disability, for example, this is not a random tragedy for which there is no explanation. Its roots are in another lifetime – a karmic debt is being worked out.

Much of the evidence for a belief in past lives comes from countries such as India and Pakistan, where it is widely accepted. Many children in these lands profess memories of recent previous existences.

In Tibet the religious leader, the Dalai Lama, is believed always to migrate from one body to the next almost immediately upon death. A major search is launched by priests to find the child who continues the existence of the soul of this great spirit. The new Dalai Lama is recognised by an ability to describe intimate details of the private life of the previous host body.

In the West however, past life research usually requires the use of hypnotic regression. In a trance a person is asked to 'remember' scenes from before they were born. About one in ten people seems able to do this and come up with rich 'memories' of a previous existence.

One of the leading experts in the field, Joe Keeton, explains that he can always tell the difference between a genuine past life memory and a fantasy. For example, if the recall is real then the person cannot communicate properly about a life lived more than a few hundred years ago. The differences in language make the questions asked incomprehensible.

Notes

One of Keeton's most intriguing cases concerns Liverpool journalist Monica O'Hara. After a series of dreams in which water played a terrifying part, she sought to explore whether they might hide a past life memory.

Indeed, that seemed to be the case. Under hypnosis Monica recalled a memory of a love affair with a young man who was disapproved of by her family. In order to escape persecution the couple chose to flee Britain and start a new life in America. They booked a passage on a ship leaving Southampton in April 1912. The ship's name was the *Titanic*.

In her past life 'memories' Monica describes the horror as the ship sank and the water claimed the lives of her boyfriend and herself. The legacy of this drowning was her phobia about water in her next incarnation.

Unfortunately, we can never be certain whether this is a real memory or just imagination. The woman and her boyfriend are not on the Titanic passenger list under the names Monica gave, though she says they booked under false names to avoid detection.

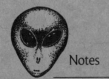

Notes

I conducted an experiment with Joe Keeton with the help of the BBC. We took a woman producer who was utterly sceptical of past lives and performed a series of regressions. Over a few weeks she gradually revealed a remarkable past life story, told in a rich accent that was nothing like her own.

In this past life the producer 'became' Jill Leadenoak, a pig farmer's daughter seemingly from medieval England. As Keeton predicted, she proved difficult to talk with. Jill knew nothing about the year or who was on the throne. All she could tell us was that she lived near 'the green wood' and the names of all her pigs!

However, Jill added a fascinating story about the brewing of cider at a local inn. The process involved dangling dead rats on strings to help in the fermentation and checks revealed that this disgusting practice was once carried out. A number of other clues also located the area to Herefordshire, a part of England the present-day woman did not know at all.

There was no record of Jill Leadenoak – she was just too mundane a character to leave a mark on history.

Things were different with Ray Bryant from Reading in Berkshire. In his past life memory he described in vivid detail the career of a Lancashire soldier called Reuben Stafford.

Stafford had served during the Crimean War and been wounded − only to be nursed back to health by 'Florrie's Ladies' − as he called the nursing staff headed by Florence Nightingale. Elaborate descriptions of battles and military uniforms were provided by Bryant during his regressions. These all checked out − as did the existence of Reuben Stafford. His service record was found in obscure notes at a barracks in Preston but had not seemingly been published in any source that Ray Bryant might have come across.

Through other sources and unbeknown to Bryant, the subsequent death of Stafford was traced. Stafford worked in the London docks and committed suicide. Bryant was asked to relive his memory of this moment. His account of the old man's tragic demise fitted perfectly with the facts.

Does this prove that Ray Bryant *was* Reuben Stafford in another lifetime? Neither he nor hypnotist Joe Keeton are certain − only that in some way the mind of a person long dead has a timeless quality to it.

Notes

Notes

One of the most astonishing past life cases involved California hypnotherapist Dr Marge Rieder. In 1986 she was approached in the small town of Lake Elsinore by a woman called Maureen Williamson.

Maureen had begun to have curious 'flashbacks' and in one she doodled the name 'John Daniel Ashford' on some paper in a crowded restaurant. Taken back in time by hypnosis Maureen described a fantastic love story set during the American Civil War more than a century before. It focused on the town of Millboro, thousands of miles from California in a state that she had never visited. The story ended in tragedy and death and these emotions had imprinted themselves across time.

However, there was an even more fantastic twist. Re-living her life as 'Becky' – wife of John Daniel Ashford in this Virginia town in 1861 – Maureen recognised others living there who were today known to her from her present life. All lived around Lake Elsinore.

One by one these were regressed and they all re-lived those days in Millboro 125 years before. It was as if a whole group of souls had been reunited in new bodies and had come together in today's incarnation.

If past life evidence relied only upon the use of hypnosis we might have cause for doubt. This method is known to stimulate the ability to fantasise. But surprisingly often people have a spontaneous memory of a previous existence.

This is notably true of very young children. Studies show that one in four seems to recall a time before they were born, although almost all lose these memories before they leave primary school.

In one stunning case two young girls from Northumberland were killed in 1957 when a driver ran off the road and tragically struck them. They apparently returned to be born as twin daughters to the same family two years later.

The Pollock twins both had memories of their earlier life. They used dolls names their dead sisters had adopted. They recognised a town that they had never visited but the other girls knew well. One had a birthmark identical to a scar one of the dead girls had acquired after a bicycle accident. The two girls were once found huddled together in a garden terrified by a car in the street which had by chance been heading in their direction. It was angled in exactly the same way as the vehicle that had struck and killed their sisters. After reaching the age of eight both girls lost all recall of their previous existence.

This case is not unique.

Notes

GHOSTS

'You look like you've just seen a ghost' is a very common expression. Yet, oddly, many people seem unaware when they *have* done just that.

Ghosts are not usually transparent, ethereal forms or floating shapes with white sheets draped over their heads, as commonly portrayed in the movies. By all accounts apparitions look like ordinary human beings and are as solid as anybody else. They are indistinguishable from you or me.

Psychics who claim to see spectral forms quite often say that most people would not be aware if they had seen one unless it happened to do something impossible – like walk through a wall – or unless they knew for certain that the person they were seeing was actually dead.

In fact, spirits allegedly surround us invisibly all of the time and most people probably see one every now and then.

So, if you are adamant that you have never seen a ghost – think again. According to those who research these matters, you probably have. You just didn't realise it at the time!

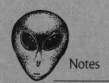

Notes

Ghosts do not always appear visually. There are reports of phantom sounds of battles held centuries ago. Spooky smells are also very common.

Linda Pezze of Torrington, Connecticut, entered her home one December day to find the gas cooker ring was lit. She knew that she had not turned it on. Next day Linda returned again and this time all of the cooker rings were lit. There was also a sweet odour of lily of the valley permeating the house.

This woman's shock soon turned to tears of joy when she realised the date. It was one year to the day since her mother's death. Her mother had always been fastidious about turning off the cooker rings before leaving the house and her favourite perfume was lily of the valley.

To Linda Pezze there was no doubt. The ghost of her mother had returned from the beyond to show that she was watching over her daughter.

Sometimes such loving attention from the departed can prove a little more awkward.

When Gillian's husband died at the age of 37 this Essex woman was left to raise a young family on her own. It was struggle but she kept his ashes in the bedroom as a permanent reminder of their bond of love. Then strange things began to happen.

There were peculiar noises in the bedroom late at night. A spectral face appeared floating beside the bed and objects began to move around the room. Gillian decided that her husband wanted his ashes to be buried and after she obliged the disturbances ceased.

But then, five years later, she met a new man and they settled down together. Suddenly one night the bed began to lift into the air — rising under the influence of an unseen force. Her new partner was terrified but Gillian sat implacably pleading into the night.

'Don't worry,' she told her companion. 'It's just my first husband.'

'But he's dead,' the man replied.

'I know. But he gets jealous,' she responded.

Next day Gillian was on her own again. Her new lover could not cope with an eternal triangle that had one side in heaven.

One curiosity is that ghosts are not always people (or animals) who are dead. There are many reliable cases of apparitions who are still very much alive.

Often these occur when the individual is in some sort of emotional or physical crisis. They may be lying on a sick bed thousands of miles away or desperately pining to be with a loved one. In these circumstances their form can sometimes be seen as if they are really present but far from where their body currently resides. Consciously they may not even realise they are traversing time and space in this way. They act like non-intelligent images – walking but not communicating with anyone who passes by.

Even more astonishing are the ghosts of non-living things.

Ghost houses, flower beds, even a spectral telephone box have all been reported. This fits the theory that apparitions are like video replays of scenes from the distant past.

There are several well-attested accounts of steam locomotives seen (or more often heard) passing through places far from a railway track – even in one case a modern housing estate. In all known examples a railway line did run through this location many years ago.

The most common type of ghostly encounter is called the 'crisis apparition'. It occurs at the moment of death and involves the form of a loved one appearing in the room — often late at night — as if they are saying goodbye on the way to the afterlife.

In one case a man from Birkenhead, in Cheshire, was shot when he disturbed car thieves while coming home from work. At that moment — several miles away — his wife heard the phone ring as she was doing the ironing. She picked it up with one hand, whilst continuing with the ironing as she spoke.

It was her husband.

'Where are you?' Lucia asked.

'I am so very far away.'

After insisting that he loved her deeply his voice faded. It was then that the true nightmare struck Lucia. Her hand was clutching empty air. There was no telephone in the room.

When the police arrived an hour later they had no need to tell her the terrible news. She already knew the awful truth because her husband had said his farewells even as his body lay dying in a town centre street.

Notes

Possibly the most remarkable reported apparition confronted a man from Birmingham who had to pay a visit to the outside toilet at his home in the middle of the night.

Opening the wooden door in the yard he stepped back in amazement to realise that the lavatory was occupied. As his eyes adjusted to the darkness an amazing sight met his gaze. For this was not what anyone would expect to encounter in their garden late at night: a Zulu warrior in full regalia and carrying a spear!

After a few moments the apparition disappeared and the Zulu was never seen again. However, there is a sequel to this story. The man's brother – a seaman – was missing at the time. He was later found, being cared for by an African tribe. Was the ghostly Zulu warrior a message that all would be well?

It is not just human beings who return as ghosts. Beloved pets often seem to re-appear to their owners.

Debra Dean of Cheshire reports how she returned home from work one day to find her poodle waiting to greet her on the doorstep.

'He ran up to say hello – just as he always did. His little tail was wagging and I bent down to stroke him.'

Then he disappeared. The dog had died several months before.

According to psychologists we can explain apparitions of this type as an example of the 'phantom limb' effect. People who have had surgery to amputate an arm or leg often report that they can still feel it for some time afterwards. This is because the body has become so used to its presence that it continues to register as if it were still there.

Is the same true for emotions? Do we sense the presence of people – and pets – whom we have known for many years because our mind takes time to adjust to their departure?

Or is there a spirit side to all of our beings that can return to this earth for a brief moment when the conditions are right?

TIMESLIPS

A timeslip is not like a dream or a vision but a real life trip through time. Bo Orsjo experienced one in June 1974. Arriving in Pasadena, California, he decided to take a hike up the bleak Mount Lowe – named after an eccentric local inhabitant. After walking for hours through mist he came upon a splendid hotel with a maid sweeping it out. The hiker was astonished to find such a place so far from civilisation. But he had brought food and drink with him, expecting to be alone, and so never entered the establishment. Later, when he told others of this curiosity they were amazed. They showed him a book about the millionaire Lowe – who had tried to build a railway to reach the summit of the mountain but had run out of money before he got there. Lowe had erected a fine hotel half-way up the slopes of the mountain that now bore his name. As a picture proved this was the place that Orsjo had visited.

But there was a problem. When Orsjo returned to the site with friends, there was no green hotel, just a few ruins. The place had been abandoned for decades and the hotel ravaged by fire – in 1937. Nothing had been on that mountainside for 37 years – yet Bo Orsjo had somehow travelled into the past to see the hotel in its heyday.

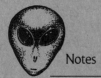
Notes

It is not only the past that can be visited during timeslips. Trips into the future can be even more incredible.

'There are some cases where we cannot know what period is represented by the timeslip. A man called D'Alessio told researcher Joan Forman how he had been walking down a suburban London street when a mistiness came over the scene and he was suddenly relocated in the future. He spent some minutes exploring this new environment to study how different things were.

Traffic was flowing silently, as if using some revolutionary motive power. It was guided by an automated system that made accidents impossible. The road surface and buildings were all glowing a strange silvery hue, and constructed of a material that was very pleasing to the eye and unlike anything he had ever seen.

Mr D'Alessio believes that the streets of London will one day look as he saw them, although perhaps his day trip had been well into the 21st century.

Belief that you have travelled through time is all very well, but has anyone ever been able to prove it?

An intriguing case involved a man called Squirrel. He was a coin collector and went to visit a shop in Great Yarmouth looking for little plastic bags in which to store his collection. As he approached the shop, however, the scene changed. The street was now cobbled and all the traffic noises disappeared.

Inside the quant interior was a woman in a long dress. She said they did sell little bags but had never heard of them being used by coin collectors. Nonetheless she agreed to sell him some for the remarkably cheap sum of 'a shilling' – which he took to mean five pence. After handing over the new coin he left the shop, noticing the shop girl staring goggle-eyed at the coin he had given to her.

The paper bag in which the little pouches were stored fell to pieces within days. The plastic rapidly turned brown but remained intact. When Mr Squirrel returned days later to buy some more there was no cobbled street, the interior of the shop had been modernised, no girl worked there and the owners could not recall ever selling the plastic envelopes.

Did Mr Squirrel travel into the past? His physical evidence might prove that: the plastic bags he bought, now obsolete, were made of cellulose like those from the early 1920s.

Notes

Undoubtedly the most amazing story of a timeslip involves two couples, the Simpsons and the Gisbeys. In October 1979 they set off from Kent to drive through Europe and decided to stop overnight at a hotel near Montélimar in the south of France.

There was a problem. No room at the inn – literally. But following directions from a strange man in a bellhop's uniform they drove along a rutted back road until they came upon a truly old-world style building adjacent to a police station.

Parking outside, they went in and booked two rooms for the night. It was a delightful place with no mod cons whatsoever. The windows had shutters, not glass. The soap was on a metal bar in the bathroom. The people even dressed in antiquated clothes. Unsurprisingly the travellers assumed that this was a 'theme' hotel.

What they did not expect were the prices charged for their bed, breakfast and evening meal, which were astonishingly low. They were also taken aback when a policeman – in old-fashioned uniform – seemed baffled by their request to be directed to the 'autoroute' (motorway).

On their return a week later the couples naturally decided to revisit this bargain hotel. But they could not find it. Then, when their holiday snaps returned, both the Simpsons and the

Gisbeys had a shock. The photographs they had taken in the hotel did not exist. It was as if they had never been there at all – even though all four of them knew that they had.

These startled people have since returned to France desperately seeking the phantom hotel. Despite assistance from the tourist board it has never been located. But the dress worn by their fellow guests as they described it has been identified and was correct – for approximately the year 1905.

Notes

SYNCHRONICITY

The term Synchronicity was coined by famous psychologist, Dr Carl Jung, who invented the concept of the collective unconscious, the idea that all living things may share images and symbols at some deep psychic level.

Jung worked in conjunction with noted quantum physicist Dr Wolfgang Pauli, who had proved how all of our physical world depended intimately on reactions that occur inside the atom. Those reactions in turn are dictated by seemingly random events – what we might call coincidence. Yet, because there are so many of them occurring every microsecond all over the cosmos, a kind of evening out is produced that creates order out of chaos and brings structure to our lives.

The theory of synchronicity argues that this same effect can be felt on all sorts of incidents in the world at large. Events that we think might be just coincidence are in fact aspects of the universe ordering itself into patterns beyond our comprehension. In other words, to seek to understand how the universe works we need to look more closely at what appear to be extraordinary coincidences.

53

A man called Jim Meadows was walking through the streets of Liverpool desperately seeking a special type of hammer that he needed for a job. But he could not find one, every shop he visited failed to come up with what he wanted.

After spending some time in sheer frustration Meadows walked along a little alleyway between stores, idly going where his feet took him while contemplating whether there was anywhere left to try.

Suddenly, out of the corner of his eye he saw something falling – it crashed to the ground just in front of him. Staring upward he could see an open window out of which it must have dropped. Whoever had been responsible had disappeared, possibly mindful of the near catastrophe that had just resulted.

Jim looked at the object and picked it up. Then he did not hesitate before walking away: it was exactly the kind of hammer for which he had been searching. Fate had conspired to resolve his dilemma. But if he had not sauntered casually down that alleyway he would not have been in the right place at the right moment.

Notes

Notes

Even the famous are not immune from the effects of synchronicity.

Oscar-winning actor Anthony Hopkins was also struggling to find something in London. He had just signed to make a movie of the book *The Girl from Petrovka* and needed a copy to work on his part. Try as he might, no book shop had it in stock.

Frustrated, he walked to the underground at Leicester Square and waited for a train. As he sat on a bench he picked up a paperback that someone had accidentally discarded. Hopkins looked around; nobody was claiming it. The book was, needless to say *The Girl from Petrovka* and he was able to prepare for the movie thanks to this good fortune.

A few weeks later he flew to Europe to commence filming. Here he met the book's author, who bemoaned the fact that he had lost his personal copy earlier that year as it had some precious margin notes. He had loaned it to a friend in London and somehow it went missing.

Hopkins' new copy had margin notes. He showed it to the author and told him the amazing story of how he had acquired it. The book was, of course, the author's original copy which by synchronicity had now returned to its rightful home across hundreds of miles.

The most extraordinary form of coincidence is what researchers call 'chain reactions'. These link countless seemingly unrelated events to point towards a major global incident.

Between November 1985 and January 1986 many such coincidences came together to provide a series of intriguingly connected clues.

A volcano erupted in Colombia. The fiery explosion melted a cap of ice, causing a catastrophic flood. Several people experienced dreams that appeared to predict this event; one even tried to warn the authorities.

Meantime, a movie appeared on British television in which a satellite called 'Vulcan' (the Roman god of fire from whom the word volcano derives) was to be used to produce floods in Colombia. The movie was made by Columbia pictures. Promotion of the movie appeared in *TV Times* magazine directly opposite a Channel 4 documentary called *The Territory Ahead* – looking at the consequences of a disaster that was expected very soon to strike the manned space programme.

At the Hotel Columbia in London a man had a dream in which he saw a rocket taking off from the eastern seaboard of the USA. His name was Max Dangerfield – possibly suggesting that the period of maximum danger had arrived.

On the US east coast, at Cape Canaveral in Florida, NASA

were struggling to launch a real rocket into space. Bad weather caused record delays preventing their shuttle 'Columbia' from taking off. As later events were to show the weather could have proved fatal. At the same time unprecedented numbers of staff were quitting the base unexpectedly.

Days afterward, on 28 January 1986, the shuttle 'Challenger' followed spaceward in just such bad weather. It was not so lucky. The mission exploded soon after take-off, killing all on board. The fire of the explosive thrusters had loosened rings weakened by ice, unleashing a devastating fiery explosion – like the one in Colombia's volcano. This chain reaction of coincidences all came together in stunning detail.

If a suitable computer programme could log all such clues could synchronicity be used to prevent tragedy? This is an idea being actively explored.

PRECOGNITION

On 14 April 1865 Julia Grant, wife of General (and future US President) Ulysses Grant had a terrible dream. She awoke full of fear that her husband was in danger and insisted that he leave Washington immediately. Grant was reluctant to agree. He had a theatre engagement that evening with President Abraham Lincoln. But his wife was so obviously distraught that he heeded her warning and they set off for the station to catch a train out of the city.

On their way by cab the couple passed a man called John Wilkes Booth. He was heading in the other direction – towards the theatre. Shortly afterwards Booth shot and killed Lincoln during the performance. It was later revealed that General Grant was also on his death list.

Lincoln's lawyer, Ward Lamon, revealed that the President had also experienced a terrible forewarning – telling Lamon about it three days earlier. In this vision Lincoln found himself wandering around the White House amidst a deathly silence. Then he came upon a coffin and heavily wrapped corpse. 'Who is dead?' he asked, to which unseen whispering voices told him, 'The president, killed by an assassin.'

Notes

Premonitions do not always happen in dreams. They can occur on the spur of the moment.

Shirley Trefoil was driving along the M62 motorway between Liverpool and Hull when a strange urge overtook her. Without giving even a moment's thought she swerved her car out of the slow lane and took it into the adjacent faster traffic flow.

'I did not look,' she explains. 'If anything had been coming close behind me it would have been disastrous.'

Moments later the truck that had been in the slow lane directly ahead of her vehicle blew a tyre. As it struggled to regain control and slowed to a halt at the roadside, its load loosened and was shed from the rear onto the motorway. Traffic behind had just enough time to avoid the deadly cargo. But had Shirley remained in position only yards behind the truck she could not possibly have escaped. Her car would have been crushed by the goods that now littered the freeway.

Something in her mind simply knew ahead of time that this event was going to happen. It did not register as a dream or a vision. It merely seized control of her body and forced her to act to save her own life.

The frustration felt by those who see the future can be immense. So it was for David Booth of Cincinnati, Ohio. For nine successive nights, from 16 May 1979, he had a vivid dream. It was always the same: he could see a plane with three engines; one was not working properly; then the aircraft crashed to the ground.

By 22 May, Booth was so certain this was some sort of premonition that he called the FAA (Federal Aviation Authority). He had identified the logo on the aircraft as signifying an American Airlines plane and pleaded with the authorities to do something – unsuccessfully. He also talked to American Airlines but nobody listened. They told him to go and see a doctor.

Days later, on 25 May, a three-engined American Airlines aircraft took off from Chicago. Moments later it lost an engine and plunged to the ground in a fireball. All 279 people on board were killed.

But that total could have been 282. One woman cancelled her trip after dreaming the night before that the plane would crash. Two other women were checking in at the airport when a terrible mood of doom overcame one of them. They re-booked onto a later flight and missed the fatal take-off.

Notes

Sceptics often ask: if a person can dream of the future why then do they not win the lottery by viewing next week's numbers? Wouldn't those who can see ahead soon be very rich? It doesn't work out like that because premonitions hardly ever occur to order. They are spontaneous and quite unexpected events.

There are cases, however, where luck in the lottery has been driven by a dream. In 1995 Margaret Bramley was awoken in the middle of the night in her house in Northern England. Her husband had been nudging her, asking why she was muttering a series of numbers in her sleep.

As she explained: 'If I had slept right through I would have probably forgotten about the dream that I had that night. But being disturbed made me remember. I was entering an extra line on my ticket – one that I did not normally use.'

Thankfully, between them the couple recalled the dream numbers and entered them that week in the lottery as an additional line. They won over £100,000.

Unfortunately, those who study cases of precognition have discovered that tragedy is foreseen more often than happy events. The key appears to be emotion. An event must have a direct impact and be vivid to the life of the person who sees into the future.

Do premonitions mean that the future is already ordained? Or can we alter what is to come?

Marilyn Mayer tells how she had a frightening dream about her ride along the expressway leading to the airport in San Francisco. She saw how the three fellow occupants of the car sat in a particular way, then they entered the freeway and were struck head on by a truck that suddenly cleared the central reservation.

That morning as planned two of her friends arrived on time, including one who was very cynical of precognition. He insisted that they sit as in the dream just to 'call the bluff' on Marilyn's story. The third passenger was late in arriving. The party set off on the expressway only to screech to a halt behind a line of traffic. Police advised them of a terrible fatal accident. It was exactly as in Marilyn's dream but had happened – just when they would have been on that stretch of road had the passenger who came late not experienced an unusual delay.

Did Marilyn see the possible future that would have occurred had the car been on time that morning? Did her friend detect the coming accident on an unconscious level and hold up their journey just enough to prevent them from becoming involved? Either way, this case suggests that the future is not immutable. We are not prisoners of fate.

Notes

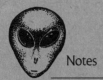
Notes

Lawrence had a powerful premonition
that something would go wrong
whilst out hunting.

In an attempt to prove the reality of precognition American researcher William Cox attempted a fascinating experiment.

He recorded the number of travellers in a certain carriage on a railway train during a number of journeys throughout the year. These were then compared with the number who travelled in that particular coach on a day when the train was subsequently involved in a crash.

The results were startling. Fewer passengers were in the fateful carriage on the day when disaster struck. It was as if some of them were aware of the coming events and had subconsciously decided to take an alternative seat on the day when the accident took place.

Odds were calculated as greater than 100 to 1 against this effect being merely the result of chance. It offers some of the best evidence we have that precognition is a real phenomenon – aside from the many thousands of case histories from people who claim to have seen the future before it happens.

Notes

Researchers believe that all of us experience a preview of the future through our dreams – perhaps more often than we realise. They claim that you can prove this to yourself by way of a dream diary.

It is suggested that you try the experiment during a period when you are doing new things – such as moving house, changing jobs or going on holiday. The way that the brain processes such novel experiences seems to trigger premonitions.

Record as many of your dreams as possible during this period, perhaps over a one week spell. Even people who claim never to dream do in fact do so for two hours every night. It is just that most of us are poor at retaining the memory after we awake. However, we can all be trained to recall more detail in the few moments immediately after waking when those dream memories are still in place.

To do this you should keep a notebook and pen by the bedside – or better still a portable tape recorder to talk into – to capture your memories. Without getting out of bed – and preferably without fully opening your eyes or sitting up in bed – describe as much as you can of the night's dreams. Recalling one image usually produces a cascade effect and many other fragments will emerge.

Study the diary at the end of the week and see whether any of the dreams match coming events. These connections are usually made within 24 to 72 hours after the dream. Only 5% of premonitions seem to concern time periods further than three days into the future.

Those who have tried these experiments claim the results can be astonishing. Many discover by this method that time does not work at all in the way we usually accept.

Mysteries of the Earth

CRYPTOZOOLOGY

There are millions of species of animals all over the planet. Some are unique to one small environment, while others are quite widespread. Sadly, each year many of these species become extinct – often due to changing planetary conditions or, more often, the intervention of man.

Although we believe that we have discovered most life forms on earth there remain huge areas to be explored – particularly in the depths of the ocean. It is not inconceivable that new creatures – even large ones – are waiting to be found.

Those who study mystery animals are known as 'cryptozoologists'. They are engaged in two principal types of research, seeking either completely new creatures (whose existence may be legendary) or those that did exist once but are believed to have been long extinct.

They also keep an eye out for what are known as 'alien animals'. Despite the name, such animals do not come from another planet. In fact the term means any creature seen living in a location where it is not supposed to exist.

Notes

Notes

Discovering real life fossils is quite possible. The huge lung fish – known to walk along the sea bed in a bizarre manner – were believed to have become extinct millions of years before the earliest humans first appeared. But then one of these creatures – known as a coelacanth – was retrieved by Indian Ocean fishermen sixty years ago. Now it is known that these animals thrive...they are just well hidden.

The same may be true of some alien animals. Wallabies (a small type of kangaroo) have never been native to Britain, but reports of them being seen in the Derbyshire Peak District are now established as fact. It appears that a small colony has evolved from a few zoo escapees a century ago.

Notes

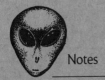

Notes

But what about big cats – such as pumas? There are countless reliable reports of these creatures being seen in remote highland areas, notably the moors of Devon and Cornwall – where the infamous 'Beast of Bodmin' has been blamed for the deaths of numerous sheep.

There have been many attempts to come up with proof. Army tracking teams have pursued the Beast. Armed police hunts have failed to find the culprit and in 1995 an investigation by the Ministry of Agriculture concluded that the creature was probably just a large dog being mistaken for something bigger and fiercer – some farmers preferred to shoot first and ask questions later.

Similar arguments were used to explain a spate of big cat sightings in Scotland – until one of the creatures was caught and killed near Kellas. It proved to be an entirely new species of wild cat that was not unlike a small version of the puma.

It is known that some people have kept big cats such as lynxes for pets and have released them when they grew too large to handle. Could these survive and even multiply in the wild?

Of all the unproven creatures perhaps the most famous is the Yeti – otherwise known as the 'Abominable Snowman'. This biped, larger than any man and covered in grey/white matted hair is said to live in the high snows of the Himalayas where very few humans ever pass.

Legends of the Yeti are found amongst the peoples of Tibet and Nepal, who insist that this 'man-beast' is a reality. A number of Western expeditions sent to climb mountains such as Everest and K2 have also come upon evidence of the creature.

Sightings are quite rare, although a number of famous mountaineers tell of how their camps were attacked, in the dead of night miles from any habitation, by some huge animal. There are also tantalising photographs showing trails of massive footprints walking up the virgin snow slopes and disappearing into the inaccessible heights.

The hunt for the Yeti is well and truly on, with several expeditions planned to try to recover absolute proof. The fear is that this mysterious creature may be on the verge of extinction.

Notes

Notes

The Yeti is not the only example of a man-like beast. Almost every remote, mountainous area of the world has legends of similar creatures – backed up by modern-day sightings. The Australians know the beast as the Yowie – a word derived from centuries-old aboriginal encounters. The Russian equivalent is the Alma. Perhaps the best known example, however, is Bigfoot – from the high-altitude regions of the USA. This creature was also known to the native Americans for hundreds of years and had been given the name of Sasquatch. Major similarities occur between all of the stories. The matted hair changes in colour in a logical manner according to the terrain – white against snow, brown against sandstone, and so on. It is as if this covering is natural camouflage developed through evolution. Those who get very close to the creature also invariably say that it has a terrible odour.

The biggest problem facing those trying to prove the reality of these man-beasts is the total absence of any bodies. There is also relatively little visual evidence – such as photographs or film. But the Bigfoot hunters are certain from many eyewitness accounts that these creatures must be real; although possibly rare, shy and sufficiently intelligent that they might even bury their dead.

Just as mountains all over the world have legends about man-beasts, so nearly all major lakes in the far northern latitudes provide stories about monsters lurking in their depths.

These enormous, humped creatures have been reported for more than a thousand years in some instances, and because lakes are relatively accessible and well frequented by visitors, visual evidence is quite widespread.

A number of localities have adopted their monsters and given them cute names to aid the tourist industry. Several lakes on the borders between Canada and the USA have endearing stories and if you tour these locations you can buy souvenirs and see plaques depicting the exploits of Champ or Ogopogo.

Impressive pieces of film showing the humps of some largely submerged creature rising to the surface and sinking again have been obtained from Japan to Scandinavia. To many the case is already proven that these animals are real. The only question outstanding is what they might be.

Sceptics are quick to point out that small waves, tree trunks and other mundanities can appear deceptive to those unfamiliar with the lake: there is no doubt that quite a few monster sightings have a down to earth explanation.

Notes

The best hope of discovering a 'lost world' filled with surviving dinosaurs seems to come from a remote area of the African Congo.

The weed-choked rivers around Lake Tele certainly had real dinosaurs over sixty million years ago and the region has changed remarkably little since those times. Even the intrusion of head-hunting pygmy tribes have done little to destroy the natural habitat and those same natives insist that a long-necked creature lives on in the river systems. They call it the mkoele mbembe.

Missionaries first heard about this creature a hundred years ago. Since then a number of expeditions by cryptozoologists have made the dangerous trek to Lake Tele and uncovered hard evidence. This includes eye-witness stories (including the alleged capture, killing and eating of one of the beasts by a local tribe during the 1950s) and physical evidence in the form of trails, huge holes in bushes and close encounters involving loud splashing sounds.

One team of scientists finally saw the creature in May 1983. It was in the water, craning its neck like a giraffe to eat the flowering liana plants from the surrounding tall trees. Carefully wading out to see it, the scientists filmed the dinosaur – not unlike a pint-sized brontosaurus. Unfortunately they forgot to eset their movie cameras after recently filming monkeys. The nkoele mbembe vanished beneath the water and on return to ivilisation the shocked scientists discovered that their film was blurred mess.

More expeditions are planned and the cryptozoologists elieve that they have a strong chance of getting absolute roof of a surviving dinosaur from what we well might call a real fe Jurassic Ark.

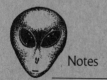

Notes

Undoubtedly the best known lake monster of all is Nessie – the creature said to inhabit Loch Ness in the north of Scotland. A whole industry has grown up promoting her. Caravans frequently mark the site of lakeside investigations. So numerous have been the witnesses and photographs that it seems easy to believe that something is down there. The loch is incredibly deep and full of peat so underwater searches have largely proven fruitless – scuppering the best hope of proving the case.

Nevertheless, there have been some intriguing results produced by sonar scans sweeping the loch, which imply that a large animal may exist. Suggestions as to what it is range from a giant eel to some form of aquatic dinosaur.

There are lakes in North America, however, where similar monster stories have actually been resolved. In one case, the culprit was exposed as a very large fish – perhaps ten feet long. Fortified by tradition and much imagination this had become exaggerated by generations of watchers into the stuff of legends.

HISTORICAL RIDDLES

How were the pyramids built? According to the traditional interpretation these huge structures, rising high above the Egyptian desert, were constructed as both tombs and monuments to a succession of pharaohs. Each ruler planned his own pyramid and employed thousands of slaves to create this vision over many years in order that it would be ready for his eventual passing to the afterlife.

There are some, however, who doubt that this technological feat was possible with the primitive facilities available thousands of years ago. They point to the engineering skills required and the precision of the astronomical alignments and the baffling underground passageways that link the various internal chambers.

In the 1960s the 'ancient astronauts' school of thought suggested that the Egyptians might have had alien help in the construction process. Was a race of wise beings from another star system here to oversee intelligent life on this planet?

Ultimately, it is a choice between whether ancient man was more clever than we can imagine (which science assures us to be the favoured option) or whether assistance was necessary – perhaps from a distant world.

During the 16th century a provincial French doctor called Michel de Notredame practised a different kind of skill: soothsaying.

Nostradamus, as he is best known today, visited the kings and noblemen of Europe making predictions which he claimed were a mixture of astrological calculation from the motions of the stars and visions sent to him by God.

His *Centuries* – a series of four-stanza verses grouped into hundreds – have acquired a fabulous reputation. The Bible is the only other book to have been continuously in print since the invention of the printing press.

Was Nostradamus a genuine mystic or a clever fraud? Unfortunately, his prophecies are couched in impenetrably archaic language and use his own brand of complex anagram. Decoding them has become an art form of dubious pedigree.

Although some of his 'centuries' appear very specific – referring to a huge fire in a city in the year 'six and sixty,' for example (arguably denoting the Great Fire of London in 1666) – the majority are vague. Even the precise verses have often been adopted by interpreters to fit in better with a new event, perhaps a hundred years after being definitively accepted as a match for something else.

In one of his most chilling verses (one of very few that names a date) Nostradamus warns of a 'great king of frightfulness' that will fall from the sky in the seventh month of the year 1999. Is he warning that the earth will be struck by a great asteroid or comet? Something similar did occur millions of years ago and as a result much of life on earth was wiped out almost overnight.

In 1917 in a small Portuguese village something remarkable took place.

A group of local children claimed that for several months they were visited in a field near Fatima by a glowing being who came from the skies. They interpreted their visitor as the Virgin Mary – although others claim that the figure acted more like an extraterrestrial! After giving the children a series of prophecies to be fulfiled during the 20th century, the figure promised a miraculous return on 17 October of that year. Word spread and tens of thousands of people flocked to the field to witness the events. Pouring rain ceased just before the appointed time and many swear that the sun 'danced' in the sky to signify the truth of what is now called the 'miracle of Fatima'. There are photographs of the crowd staring awestruck at the sky but no reliable proof of the miracle. Was it mass hysteria or self-hypnosis? Did an optical illusion distort the sun? Could an alien spacecraft have hovered overhead? Or was it truly a sign from God?

The first Fatima prophecies were allegedly fulfiled with the World Wars and the Russian revolution. But the final one – said to be the most horrific of all – has been hidden by the papacy ever since. They have declined requests to reveal its content – although time is definitely running out.

Notes

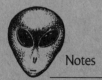

Notes

Throughout the centuries there have been reports of statues and other religious artifacts that have suddenly become infused with life. Shrines have been set up around the locations of these 'miracles' and they are revered even to this day. These miracles have continued in the present century. During the 1970s a number of statues in Ireland were seen to move about of their own volition and this brought media from around the world to the small grotto at Ballinspittle in an attempt to capture the phenomenon on camera. More recently there have been numerous reports of 'crying' statues, where tears appear to form in the eyes of plaster models. In some cases it has been the porous material used to create the statue, which absorbs water and then sheds it again according to fluctuations in the ambient conditions. But this has not explained every incident. The most astonishing events have occurred at Belmez de la Moraleda, a small Spanish village. In 1971 a number of human faces appeared over a period of several days 'etched' onto flagstones in one of the tiny houses. Apparently bleached into the stone by water and chemicals, these have continued to form and then gradually fade away again despite surveillance of the area. The cause of this extraordinary series of events remains a mystery.

Notes

FALLS FROM HEAVEN

One of the strangest words you will come across in the wo[rld]
of the paranormal is fafrotsky. This is the shortened form of
'falls from the sky'.

As you will see, all manner of oddities have been known to
tumble from the heavens and descend to earth as fafrotskies.

The two obvious questions faced by researchers striving to
figure them out is where these objects come from – and how
they got to where they did.

The Barrett family of West Kirby in Cheshire were watching television one evening when they heard a whistling noise that lasted a few seconds. Then there was a sudden crash and the whole house shook. Rushing upstairs they found part of their roof had collapsed and a mass of ice was sitting on the bed. It was more than a foot across and had a pale blue colour.

Ice bombs like this are not uncommon. Several fall somewhere in the world every year and they vary in size from giant hailstones to potentially lethal masses. There are reliable accounts of animals being killed and one unconfirmed case from Germany of a rooftop worker skewered by an icy fafrotsky in 1951. Thankfully the vast majority do no damage. It is often suggested that ice bombs fall from aircraft with fault toilet systems or where de-icing equipment has failed. But examples are on record from before the invention of aircraft.

In April 1973 a physicist from Manchester University was startled when an ice bomb plunged onto the street. He took it for analysis and discovered that it had descended tens of thousands of feet through the atmosphere, gathering layer after layer of ice in the process. It had no fewer than fifty-one coatings and was like a giant rounded icicle.

Notes

Falls of ice are one thing, but the most extraordinary kind of fafrotsky is when living animals are dropped from the sky. There has been a remarkable array of examples – fish are often cited.

On 23 October 1987 a shower of tiny living frogs was deposited on the ground at Stroud in Gloucestershire. Scientific identification of the specimens revealed an even more amazing fact. This variety came from the African desert. How had they travelled thousands of miles?

Speculation is that such creatures might be sucked up in water droplets during a tornado or sandstorm to be carried like incredible hitch-hikers high in the clouds. Yet how they could survive such a journey is difficult to imagine.

As a result, an even more weird theory proposed by some researchers is that the animals are teleported from one spot to another by an unknown mechanism. One moment a shoal of fish might be swimming in the Adriatic – seconds later it could be falling from the sky on a street in east London.

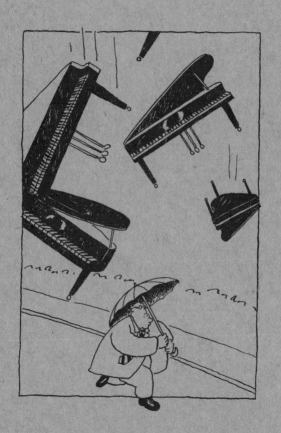

Notes

In the Bible the most famous fafrotsky case of all time was reported when an edible mass called 'manna' fell from heaven to feed the starving multitude.

Organic conglomerations of this kind (sometimes even edible ones) have been reported to descend in more recent times – ranging from a huge blob of goo that fell on an Ontario town to pools of tar that soaked Louisiana fields.

But even more astonishing things have fallen as well. One of the strangest cases occurred outside a church in Cheshire. It literally rained money, when coins of small denominations fell with a shower of rain and left startled passers-by scrambling for souvenirs.

Where these coins came from remains a total mystery.

The most gigantic example of an object to fall from above was in June 1908, when a fiery ball was seen to crash from the skies over northern Europe. It exploded in mid-air above the Siberian tundra in the vicinity of the Tunguska river.

Such was the ferocity of this explosion that it felled trees for hundreds of square miles as if they were pins in a bowling alley. Reindeer were burned to a crisp by the heat and only many years later did the similarities with a nuclear blast become apparent. However, there are no naturally occurring nuclear explosions and mankind did not invent this type of weapon until 37 years later.

Huge quantities of dust were cast into the atmosphere by what was the biggest single explosion in modern history. For days afterwards people were able to read newspapers in the dead of night as far away as London because the dust scattered and reflected light.

Expeditions to the tundra later found a scene of mass destruction but no trace of the vast meteorite that most scientists assumed caused this devastation.

So what did fall over Tunguska? Scientists today think it could have been a small comet that vapourised with enormous energy miles above the ground. But eyewitness accounts say that the object changed course shortly before the explosion –

something a comet could not have done. This has led to some speculation that a nuclear-powered alien spacecraft may have crashed to earth.

We may never know the truth.

Notes

STRANGE ENERGIES

Much of northern Europe, especially the British Isles, is covered with the remains of fantastic stone circles, of which the massive site at Stonehenge is the most famous.

Mystery shrouds the question of why heavy rocks were transported over long distances to build what many believe were either religious shrines or astronomical calendars to help farmers know when to plant crops.

But modern research has shown that these stones appear
ossessed of a hidden energy. The 'Dragon Project' has for
ome years used sensors to detect radio and electrical signals
manating from the large standing stones at various sites –
specially at sunrise and sunset. It has been suggested that
hese signals might be derived from a power held within the
arth itself.

Were these monuments built at focal points of the earth's
nergy to channel these forces into the stones?

Notes

Studies have shown that certain types of rock – particularly those containing quartz crystal – can squeeze out an electrical signal when put under pressure. This means that, in locations where there are reservoirs or other quarries (to press down on the rock) and tall masts or chimneys to channel the subsequent release of energy, huge outflows are possible.

Normally this power is invisible, although it can lead to tingling sensations and other electrical effects on passers-by. However, at what are called 'window areas' this energy can be so strong as to trigger a chain reaction in the atmosphere and under certain conditions create a floating ball of glowing light – known as a plasma.

Experiments pressurising rocks in the laboratory and filming them with high-speed cameras have proven the viability of these theories. Researcher Paul Devereux calls the large-scale plasmas (perhaps several feet in diameter) by the name of earthlights and believes that they might be mistaken for UFOs as they float freely around hilly areas.

Numerous 'window area' sites have been discovered all over the world where such floating lights have been reported for many centuries. These were often regarded as signs from the gods in the legends of ancient cultures.

Another phenomenon linked to these leaks of energy was first identified by the Victorians and named the 'Humadruzz'. This was a mysterious sound combining buzzing, humming and droning that was heard in the dead of night. Some imaginative commentators thought it might come from a race of trolls living underground and using mining equipment!

In those days there was no domestic electricity so this source – often blamed for modern outbreaks of what is now more simply called 'The Hum' – could not have been responsible. 'The Hum' is just as common today: it plagues certain areas for weeks on end and then suddenly disappears for long periods. It has driven people out of their houses in despair – although neighbours claim to have heard nothing. The few audio recordings made prove that it is a real effect and not a psychological phenomenon. British government studies in the 1960s, failed to prove that it was caused by hearing defects, as sceptics suggested.

Reports of the mysterious humming have come from all over the world and it is now believed that it may be an audible consequence of earth energies issuing from rocks at 'window area' sites. In effect, it is the sound of our living planet.

Notes

Notes

t is not only the planet that can be charged with electrical energy. A human being can also become a living battery.

There are many reports of so-called 'office jinxes' – people who cause computers and fax machines to malfunction as soon as they go near them, and who can get electrical shocks simply from touching metal objects. There are vivid accounts of the 'electric kiss': a shock can occur when the lips of one of these individuals touch somebody else's.

Our bodies abound with electricity and most people notice minor examples of these effects. Studies at Oxford University, however, have shown that these 'electric people' store ten times more energy than normal. This can have alarming results and many of the worst sufferers go through numerous domestic appliances like vacuum cleaners and washing machines as leaking body energy causes them to blow circuits time after time!

This phenomenon remains far from understood – not least in some extreme cases where the affected person has been known to glow in the dark.

A destructive form of energy that is still a mystery is ball lightning. Despite its name it seems unconnected with ordinary lightning and often forms when there is no thunderstorm activity.

Ball lightning is scientifically accepted, although until the 1960s it was considered by many physicists to be just as ridiculous as alien spaceships. It is still more likely to be reported to a UFO investigator than to a university department.

The phenomenon varies in colour (blue and orange are common) and size (from an inch to several feet in diameter). Its shape is round, or tubular and it floats freely in the atmosphere. However, ball lightning does not form only out in the open. It has been reliably reported emerging from cookers and TV sets, creeping down chimneys and drifting around living rooms for several seconds – even on one occasion moving down the aisle of a passenger airliner in front of many startled witnesses.

There is huge energy bottled up in ball lightning. In well-attested cases it has melted metal and instantaneously evaporated a barrel of water. Yet, paradoxically, it has also been known to pass right through human bodies causing only minor side effects.

Because of these huge discrepancies in the evidence nobody yet understands how ball lightning forms or what kind of energy comprises. But in several countries the race is on to be the first to harness the fantastic power trapped within this natural phenomenon.

One day in January 1985 a teenage girl was walking down the stairs at a Cheshire college laughing with some friends. Moments later she was a human fireball which, although rapidly extinguished, tragically claimed her life a few days later. Attempts to find a possible cause for this incident led to several speculations – the idea, offered by one firefighter, that she had spontaneously combusted being the most weird.

Of all strange phenomena most people find spontaneous human combustion – or SHC – by far the most chilling. It leaves one with a sense of absolute helplessness.

Eyewitness observations are very rare. More common is the discovery of the remains of a human body within a pile of ash some hours after that person was seen alive and well. Typically, part of a hand or foot may be left to aid in identification but every other part of the body will be totally consumed. Yet, incredibly, the surrounding area in the room is often barely touched. SHC victims have been found on top of plastic tiles that were not even warped.

Notes

Notes

Evidence strongly suggests that the fire involved in spontaneous human combustion starts somewhere inside the body and, unless immediate help is on hand, can burn so fiercely and yet in such a localised manner that bones are turned to powder in a way that never occurs in an ordinary fire death.

SHC remains highly controversial. Many scientists refuse to accept that it can be real. But fire officers who have attended a case say the proof is in the site photographs.

Theories range from the possibility that high levels of body electricity can set off a chain reaction inside the digestive system when combustible gases are in excess, to the terrifying image of ball lightning forming inside the body and burning its way outwards with its searing power.

For most of us the very idea is just too awful to contemplate.

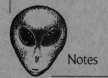

Notes

CROP CIRCLES

There can be few people who have never seen a crop circle – either in a field of grain or through the colourful photographs on television or in books. It is the greatest new mystery of the modern age. But appearances can be very deceptive.

The first cases to which the term 'crop circle' was applied occurred in oat fields in Wiltshire in August 1980. They were large single expanses of crop which were swirled flat. Although the ground inside the circle was gently layered in a spiral shape, the cut-off point was sharp and grain stood erect at the circle edge, blending into the rest of an undamaged field.

These 1980 cases were not perfect circles. Indeed, the farmer thought that the wind was to blame and quickly harvested his crop. Whilst a further sprinkling of circles occurred in Hampshire and Wiltshire during the next few summers and were investigated by a band of enthusiasts it was to be a decade before the world at large really discovered there was a mystery.

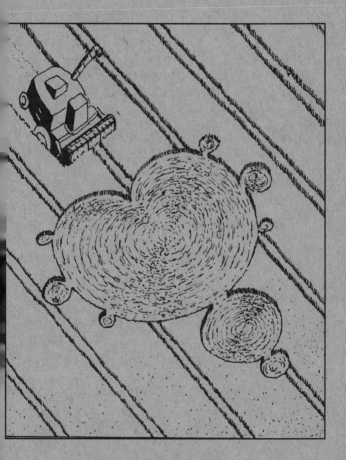

The development that brought international fame for the crop circles was the discovery of what came to be known as 'pictograms'. The hundreds of circles that formed during the summer of 1989 included several of far more stunning complexity than before which seemed undoubtedly to be the work of some kind of intelligence. They involved whole formations of different sized circles, straight lines and corridors, producing incredible forms that filled large areas of field.

Publication of a book called *Circular Evidence*, with many stunning photographs of pre-1989 circles and theories about possible alien forces responsible for the marks, had brought the crowds flocking to the West Country to see what all the fuss was about. Were the pictograms playing to this new influx of tourists?

Notes

CONTACT

Is there anybody out there? This question has been directed into the ether for much of the 20th century as we have strived to find our galactic neighbours and prove that we are not alone.

Even before modern times, since mankind first looked up at the stars and wondered, we have questioned whether this is the only planet where life may be found. The universe could be teeming with other civilisations just as desperate to find us in the wilderness of space.

What we do know is that every star we see in the sky is a sun just like our own. Some are far bigger and hotter. Others are like feeble candles flickering in the dark void. Most are not very different at all and each potentially has many planets encircling it – some of which could be the home of life.

The number of stars is immeasurable. We can only see a tiny fraction and the cosmos appears to go on forever. So many are the possible variations that few scientists doubt the almost certainty that there is alien life out there. And, of course, it may wish to get in contact with us.

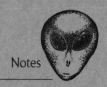

Notes

143

Notes

How can we hope to discover whether there are other civilisations? At present our technology is too limited. Although we have sent rockets to the moon and probes to the distant reaches of our solar system – sometimes making a journey of a decade or more, to take that next leap towards the final frontier is akin to contemplating a 26,000 mile walk that will circumnavigate the globe.

Even at the best possible speed that we can generate it would take a multi-billion dollar rocket ship thousands of years just to reach the nearest star – Proxima Centauri four light years away. To go further and explore the most hopeful stellar abodes for life would involve journeys of inconceivable length. By the time our distant descendants had turned around and made the voyage home our entire civilisation may well have disappeared.

One day we may invent a way to by-pass these problems and make such a trip less than impossible. For now, we can only search the universe for some sign of alien communication. It's reasonable to imagine that because we have radio so too might another intelligence out there. We can turn our instruments towards the stars, tune in, listen and hope that we might hear someone talking.

For forty years now we have been doing just that.

Notes

Sadly, our attempts to eavesdrop on cosmic chatter have been very disappointing. The hiss of natural energies fills the galaxy but is not accompanied by any obvious messages from other civilisations.

It is far more difficult to seek out alien radio broadcasts than to look for a needle in a haystack. There are trillions of places to point your receiving dish and an almost infinite number of frequencies to tune into. Vast sums of money and much of the world's energy resources would have to be spent on a full-time basis to mount a search with any reasonable hope of success. Instead we are trusting to luck that we find the right place to look.

But how do we know aliens use radio? It is limited by the speed of light – which means that if you say hello to another planet you will not hear their 'instant' reply for more than a decade because it takes the signal that long to traverse space. A century from now we may have found a method which alien races use to talk to one another. Our primitive attempts will seem like someone in New York trying to talk to a colleague in London using two tin cans and a long piece of string.

For one brief moment in the 1970s, however, it seemed as if we had succeeded. An American radio telescope picked up signals that appeared non-random. Nobody could decipher what the message was saying and, despite listening out in the same place for a long time afterwards, it never recurred.

Even so the astronomers summed up the impact of this amazing signal by scribbling on the paper that had traced out the eerie pattern just one word in big black letters – WOW!

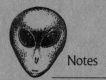
Notes

It is considered very unlikely that intelligent life could exist on any of the planets in our solar system other than earth. The environmental conditions are simply not suitable. However, the odds are rising that primitive life may be found on Mars, thanks to recent discoveries.

When 'Viking' probes soft-landed there in 1976 they found strange reactions in the rusty soil that possibly imitated the chemistry of life. Test results have also confirmed that there is water – one of the basic necessities for life – trapped as ice in parts of the Martian surface. More importantly, it was shown that running water – in the form of rivers – flowed on Mars perhaps a few million years ago, strongly implying that the planet was more earth-like at that time.

During our missions into space there have been a few occasions when it seemed as if aliens might be watching us.

In 1965, whilst drifting in a tiny space capsule high above Hawaii, astronaut James McDivitt spotted an object like a beer can that was tailing his Gemini flight. He took photographs of this unidentified companion but on landing neither he nor NASA were able to find the crucial evidence. It had disappeared from the thousands of images returned to earth.

More recently, in September 1991, a shuttle mission involving the spacecraft 'Discovery' shot remarkable video footage of incredibly high-speed objects skimming across the rim of the earth's atmosphere. They have never been explained and some scientists wonder if our quest to reach the stars is under observation.

Notes

Then a rock was discovered in the polar ice. This was a meteorite that had crashed to earth long ago, but its origin was the planet Mars. It was a chip off the planet sent hurtling through space after a violent collision, which by chance had found its way to our world.

Inside this meteorite were discovered what seemed to be fossil remains. The organism was primitive and not like anything on earth. In August 1996 NASA announced the probability that this life was from Mars: that millions of years ago bacterial organisms existed on the red planet.

Did they expand into plants and animals, as did life on earth? Are these forms still present on Mars today? Several rocket missions with sophisticated robot devices have been hastily sent on their way to find out. We may soon know if there really is life on Mars.

One stunning piece of evidence implies that intelligent beings may once have lived on Mars. During the 1976 landing missions extraordinary photographs were sent back to earth.

The pictures come from a Martian plain pockmarked with craters and known as Cydonia. Staring out from the sunlit shadows was what appeared to be a face – humanoid in form, with a hairline, two eyes, a nose and a mouth.

The image was discovered by NASA researchers who likened the face to that of the Egyptian Sphinx, carved out of rock and angled skyward to call attention to the fact that someone was there. But, even though one mile across, the face could never have been seen by telescopes on earth. We had to go to Mars to find it – as if it were an extraterrestrial calling card meant for the eyes of spacefaring passers-by.

To NASA it is simply an illusion, caused by the sunlight and shade bouncing off rocks. Other scientists are intrigued. Computer studies have revealed further detail that has not reduced the impact, as it was expected to do, but has instead enhanced the appearance of the image as a real face. This is one mystery that will quickly be resolved. The first modern spacecraft to get to Mars will take photographs to prove once and for all whether the face is an artificial monument built by an alien race or merely an optical illusion.

Notes

Notes

UFOs

The Roman army fought bravely as the sound of clashing swords rose into the skies. Suddenly there was a shriek and the noises of battle were muted. All eyes were raised towards heaven, to meet a most extraordinary sight. Hovering directly above was a huge shield, the colour of golden fire, hanging above the killing fields in silent witness.

This is one of the oldest recorded instances of a UFO sighting. Not only the Romans, but also the Greeks and many other ancient cultures saw strange things like this in the sky more than 2000 years ago.

Today we would regard them as 'flying saucers' and think about the possibility of an alien invasion. In those days they were considered to be signs from the gods and were always described in contemporary fashion, just as our modern observers interpret them as part of the space age.

There are accounts of blazing shields, fiery lances and glorious helmets shining with the power of the sun itself. For centuries these sightings were recorded in the annals, by scholars and monks. In the late 1990s they still confound the planet.

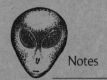
Notes

In 1896 the world stood on the threshold of a new era – that of flight.

Balloons had successfully travelled moderate distances and airships were the dream of science fiction writers such as Jules Verne, though they had yet to be perfected in working reality.

That autumn, however, incredible flying objects were seen by many people across the western United States. They resembled long cigars with boxes attached. It appeared as if someone had indeed built an amazing airship.

By April 1897 these objects were also seen in the mid-Western skies. In Texas and Nebraska there were even reports of landings. The craft came down and mysterious inventors emerged to announce that the world would soon learn of their expertise.

Of course, we never did. The apparent airships were UFOs mimicking the technology of the day. They were to appear during the next decade over Australia, New Zealand and Britain. In 1912 the Minister for the Admiralty, Winston Churchill, became the first politician to ask a question in government about these unexplained flying objects.

The UFO mystery had well and truly arrived.

Something told the aliens
there might be discord
on planet earth.

Notes

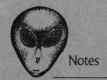

Notes

It was a bright, sunny afternoon on 24 June 1947. Kenneth Arnold, a businessman, was flying his one-engined light plane across the northwestern USA when he caught sight of a formation of crescent-shaped objects moving across the peaks of the Cascade Mountains. He measured them passing Mount Rainier and calculated an unbelievable speed.

Upon landing he reported his sighting. But aviation commentators knew these were not American aircraft, as Arnold had assumed. Nobody had any idea what they were. The pilot described them as bouncing through the air — 'like a saucer skipping across water' — meaning that they flew like a flat stone being catapulted across the surface of a lake.

He did *not* mean that they were shaped like saucers, but an enterprising reporter coined the headline-catching phrase 'flying saucer' and millions of Americans began to look for such things. Many were to see them. However, UFOs (as they were soon renamed — meaning 'unidentified flying objects') have always appeared in a rich variety of forms, of which the saucer is far more popular in space fiction movies than it has ever been in reality.

Within days of Arnold's sighting – in early July 1947 – one of the most controversial UFO incidents in history occurred on a desert ranch fifty miles outside the town of Roswell, New Mexico.

Following a thunderstorm and a mysterious explosion, landowner 'Mac' Brazel found a field strewn with shiny metal debris. A huge scar was gouged into the red soil. The wreckage itself was incredible: although light and flexible, it could not be dented with a sledgehammer. Peculiar markings were etched onto the side, almost like Egyptian hieroglyphics. Some days later Brazel took samples into town and the US Air Force base was called in to investigate. As intelligence officer Jesse Marcel collected the fantastic material his base told the world: a flying saucer had crashed.

Within minutes of the news hitting the wires and being carried around the planet the Pentagon stepped in. It was all a big mistake, they explained. The debris came from a weather balloon but nobody on the Roswell base had correctly identified what it was. The media were silenced, but when he retired thirty years later Major Marcel decided to tell the real truth about the Roswell incident. The weather balloon story was a deliberate lie. The base had been ordered into silence. They really did capture a UFO.

Notes

What crashed at Roswell?

Over the years many stories have surfaced – some even claiming that small bodies with large heads were picked up from the desert and proved to be extraterrestrial.

We do know that the weather balloon story certainly was a ruse. The remains found were taken to the 'Foreign Technology Division' of the Wright Patterson Air Force Base in Ohio, where a few months later a government project to investigate UFOs was set in motion. These facts have been verified by the release of once top secret documents.

In 1995 a British rock video producer announced that he had purchased film of autopsies being performed on the Roswell aliens. His source was an anonymous US military cameraman who had held on to the evidence for nearly fifty years. The highly contentious material was screened all over the world, but the footage does not match the descriptions of bodies found at Roswell and most leading UFO researchers, whilst accepting the sincerity of its current owner suspect the film to be of dubious origin.

An independent probe into government documents launched by a US Senator found that key Roswell files had vanished. However, the US Air Force decided to 'come clean' and explain that the crashed object was a top secret project known as

'Mogul' which was being used to search for evidence of Soviet nuclear tests.

Many UFOlogists still think the cover-up goes on and that the Roswell object really was an alien spacecraft.

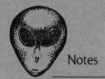
Notes

Not all UFOs are possible visits by extraterrestrials. Some appear to be unusual natural phenomena.

Researchers have spent much time in sub-zero temperatures studying strange lights that have for years flown above the remote Hessdalen valley near the Arctic Circle in Norway. The glowing forms had perplexed local villagers but experiments have established much about them.

Using radar, lasers and spectographs, UFOlogists with 'Project Hessdalen' proved that a gaseous glow known as a plasma is floating about the hills. It drifts along magnetic currents and certainly looks very spooky to the untrained eye.

Spectacular photographs of the Hessdalen lights show similarities with other spots around the world also 'haunted' by UFOs – such as the region around Marfa in Texas, mountains in the far north of Queensland in Australia and the Pennine Hills of England. When we can fully understand the mechanism generating these UFOs we may be able to tap a new power source.

After dropping off some canteen workers at 3am on 9 March 1977 two factory employees from the town of Nelson experienced what UFOlogists call a 'close encounter'.

Dropping down from clouds above the dark peak of Pendle Hill, once the notorious home of Lancashire witches, came an extraordinary cylinder glowing with light. It descended to rooftop height and hovered above the car. As it did so the engine and the lights failed.

Desperately trying to escape, the two workers struggled to restart the car engine but then gave up and fled. A weird force was pushing down on them from above and their hair was standing on end. After several horrifying minutes the floating object hummed like a generator and drifted away. Car engine and lights both came back to life on their own.

Such a 'vehicle interference' incident is one of over a thousand well-researched cases from all over the world. In several, diesel-engined vehicles have continued to operate whilst petrol-engined cars or trucks were rendered immobile. This suggests that an unknown energy impedes the flow of electrical circuits.

As yet no scientist has been able to work out how the UFOs cause these things to happen.

Notes

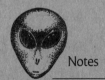

Notes

Possibly the most extraordinary close encounter occurred in a quiet pine forest eight miles from Ipswich in Suffolk, on 26 December 1980. Many people saw a glowing object fall from the sky into the woods, leaving a gaping hole in the tree canopy and triangular indentations on the frozen ground.

A patrol from the US Air Force base at Woodbridge went into the forest to investigate and confronted a conical object resting on the ground and emitting a powerful force field. All time and space in its immediate vicinity seemed to become seriously distorted. It was like wading through treacle trying to get close to it. Then it took off in a flash of light, sending local wildlife into a frenzy.

The investigation of this case by British and American authorities revealed startling evidence. The object was tracked on several radar systems, outstripping our best jet aircraft. The radiation that was scattered over the forest was many times greater than any left in the UK after the Chernobyl nuclear reactor explosion.

This case remains one of the most significant on record.

Arguments rage over what UFOs might be.

Sceptics insist it is all down to wishful thinking and misperception.

UFOlogists agree that they can explain 95% of all sightings in mundane terms. They are cases of mistaken identity involving aircraft lights, or laser light shows bouncing off clouds, or countless other strange things that do look very odd to the uninitiated.

However, about a hundred sightings occur on earth every year which defy explanation. Are these the ships of extraterrestrials visiting our planet?

Some are certainly not, being unusual natural manifestations that science will one day understand. They reflect phenomena that are presently unrecognised in the world around us – just as rainbows seemed supernatural before we came to understand how they form.

Yet in a few cases something more seems to be responsible – appearing in the form of a craft that is under intelligent control. Those who doubt that aliens are coming here do nevertheless note the long history of such sightings. To them UFOs may be timeships piloted by our future descendants exploring their distant past. And, of course, their past may well include our present day!

Notes

MEN IN BLACK

Albert Bender created one of the worlds first UFO groups – the International Flying Saucer Bureau. But in 1953 he closed down the American branch overnight and quit all of his research forever, announcing that he had been ordered into silence by three men dressed in black.

These mysterious visitors – known in UFO lore as the MIB (men in black) – claimed to be government agents who thought that Bender was getting too close to discovering the truth. They arrived in a big dark car, wearing formal suits and sporting sunglasses, and looked like gangsters from a Humphrey Bogart movie. They told him that if he did not obey their orders they would make him suffer.

Bender agreed to remain silent and during the next few years several other pioneer UFOlogists quit in equally mysterious circumstances. The legend grew that these MIB were government intimidators who ensured that the truth about UFOs would never emerge.

Notes

That there is a conspiracy to hide the truth is a key part of the UFO story, according to its researchers. They allege that, since the recovery of an alien spacecraft at Roswell in 1947, the American government has desperately tried to unravel its extraterrestrial technology. But it is so far advanced that they have the same problem that magicians in King Arthur's court would have faced had Concorde appeared in their midst.

In order to be first to grasp the fantastic secrets of the UFO the powers-that-be must prevent witnesses with important evidence from speaking out. The MIB serve as agents of the cover-up who confiscate vital material and threaten key witnesses into silence. By 1967 there were so many reports in the USA of strangers demanding evidence be handed over that the US government ordered an investigation. Thanks to the US Freedom of Information Act we have the documentation, which shows that US Air Force personnel were told to be on the lookout for MIB visiting witnesses and pretending to be government workers.

Today the MIB regularly appear as sinister protectors of the cover-up in TV series such as *The X-Files*.

An extraordinary MIB case occurred in Britain in May 1964.

A fireman took some photographs of his daughter during a picnic in a marshy area in Cumbria. When they were developed the background on one shot appeared to show the form of a spaceman.

Baffled by this fluke picture, the fireman contacted the Ministry of Defence. Then two men arrived at his home, claiming to be from the government. They interrogated him, oddly referring to one another by numbers – never by name. They drove him to the marsh in a large dark car and became angry when he refused to accept their version of events – that he had photographed an ordinary man – leaving him to walk five miles home alone. Later film taken at the site was confiscated by the Ministry as part of an investigation into a top secret matter involving the launch of a British space rocket.

The truth has never been told, but the Ministry of Defence insist that they have never sent anybody to visit a witness or to order their silence. Nor have they confiscated any film evidence.

So who were the men with no names who went to see this Cumbrian fireman and did precisely that?

Notes

ALIENS

There are hundreds of attested cases of what researchers call 'Close Encounters of the Third Kind'. These do not just involve the sighting of a UFO – but also of alien beings.

One of the earliest reports occurred a few days after the Roswell incident in 1947 – but was reported long before any claims about extraterrestrial bodies being recovered from that encounter. The sighting happened in the Italian Alps near Villa Santina and befell a terrified prospector and earth scientist.

As the Professor walked up a ravine he spotted a metal object in some rocks. Nearby were several youths whom he assumed were fellow hikers. He lifted up his geologist's pick to wave at them and then the full horror struck home. These were not teenage boys, but small sized-men with pasty faces and huge rounded eyes.

Possibly assuming the geologist was making a hostile gesture, one of the beings fired a light at him from an instrument on his belt. Immediately the scientist was thrown back down the slope, crashing into rocks and injuring himself. When he recovered his senses the aliens had gone.

But tales of contact with extraterrestrials had just begun.

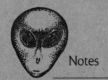

Notes

An early – and sociable – meeting with aliens involved a Wisconsin farmer known as Joe Simmonton.

He claims that a strange object landed in his garden and one of the small but human-like beings that emerged indicated the need for water. Simmonton rushed off to fill a pitcher and in return was offered some food cooking on a griddle inside the UFO. He took three of what appeared to be pancakes before the doors closed and the object shot skywards.

Simmonton ate one of the alien fast food items. He says it tasted like cardboard. The other two were analysed by researchers and turned out to be a largely inedible concoction of grease and flour. Evidently culinary skills are not an extraterrestrial strong point.

Nor, it seems, is music. A few years later the Scottish singer who entered the Eurovision Song Contest for Britain claimed that his tune – 'Only the Light' – was inspired by an alien encounter. This music of the spheres may have been top of the pops on Alpha Centauri but it was beaten into thirteenth place in the Euro-wide competition.

During the 1960s many alien sightings involved what appeared to be attempts at exploration – mirroring what we were then doing in our flights to the moon.

In July 1965 French lavender farmer Maurice Masse noticed crop disappearing from his land at Valensole. So when he saw an odd-looking helicopter on his farm and some nearby youths inspecting his plants he set off to confront them.

As soon as Maurice got close enough he could see that these were small men with egg-shaped heads and huge, rounded eyes. One of them picked up a tube attached to its waist and fired a beam of light at the farmer. He was knocked senseless. When he came to the UFO was streaking into the sky.

At the point on the ground where the UFO had landed a darkened circle later appeared. For years afterwards Masse could not get his lavender to grow properly in this place.

Notes

The descriptions of aliens met during close encounters are remarkably consistent. Well over half of the reports tell of pale-skinned beings about four and a half feet tall with a dome-shaped head, no facial hair and large eyes. They tend to wear one-piece coverall uniforms and to act aggressively towards witnesses, although never causing serious injury. It is as if they wish to keep them out of the way whilst they continue with their work.

These aliens — which dominate American UFO cases but are less common elsewhere — are known as the 'grays' because of the pigmentation of their skin. They behave like explorers and there are marked similarities with how we study animals in the wild — often stunning the subjects, taking samples for analysis and not getting too close for fear of the creatures' dangerous instincts.

Are we the equivalent of a pride of lions to these visiting extraterrestrials?

In Europe another type of entity has been more frequently encountered. They are given the name 'Nordics' because their appearance is not unlike that of Norse gods.

Nordics are much taller – often being in excess of six feet – and have long, blond, even white, hair, as well as pale skins and eyes that are slanted in a vaguely oriental manner.

Unlike the 'grays' these Nordics rarely stun witnesses and behave more like magicians – seemingly able to materialise and dematerialise and perform other incredible psychic feats.

In quite a number of cases both types of entity have appeared together. On such occasions it is always the Nordics who are in charge, with the smaller beings acting like robots trained to perform menial tasks.

A Venezuelan surgeon visited by the Nordics in 1965 was told to watch out for the smaller aliens – who were not allegedly so kindly disposed towards humanity as the tall ones. The 'grays' supposedly came from the Orion nebula and had their own agenda on earth!

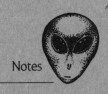

Notes

197

ABDUCTION

Seeing an alien at a distance would undoubtedly be frightening, but a terrifying new phenomenon appeared in the late 1950s. Witnesses claimed that they were being abducted.

One of the earliest examples of what are today known as 'spacenappings' involved Betty and Barney Hill, a couple from New England who in September 1961 were returning from a Canadian vacation. As they drove through the White Mountains they were followed by a banana-shaped object. Barney watched this through binoculars and says that inside it human-like beings stood behind large windows looking out at the couple.

After arriving home the Hills noticed that there was a large chunk of time unaccounted for. Their return trip had taken several hours too long. They also began to have nightmares in which a face with eyes like those of a cat kept appearing as they lay paralysed in a strange room.

In a state of alarm, the Hills went to see a doctor in Boston. He suggested that regression hypnosis be employed to get them to relive the events of their journey home.

Notes

Hypnosis is a very controversial technique. Its use in retrieving 'past life' memories has demonstrated the problems. Could it successfully unravel the missing time in the Hills' traumatic journey?

Both Betty and Barney were separately regressed by Dr Benjamin Simon over a period of several months. They each told a chilling story of how their car was stopped and they were lured towards the landed UFO before being abducted aboard by small men with pale faces and slanted eyes. Once inside a white room they were probed and examined by these entities.

The beings seemed fascinated by the fact that Betty was Caucasian and Barney dark skinned. His false teeth baffled them too. However, Betty suffered the greatest indignity – having a long needle painfully inserted into her navel with the explanation that this was a 'pregnancy test'.

Betty was not pregnant and the test made no sense. But years later a similar method was developed by doctors to extract samples of ova and test for birth defects. Other women who say they have been spacenapped allege that the taking of ova samples was indeed what the aliens were doing.

But why were they performing such procedures on humans?

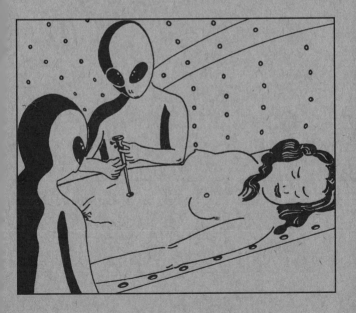

Notes

Susan, from Adelaide, South Australia, is one of the many women to have claimed repeated abductions, dating from childhood. Over 2000 cases are now on record.

The little beings who spacenapped this young woman treated her without compassion but never unkindly and explained that they were seeking to create a hybrid between human and extraterrestrial DNA. This would result in an 'alien baby' being born aboard a UFO.

Similar extraordinary tales have been told by many others and some – like Susan – have an even more incredible sequel to describe. After one abduction, during which samples were taken from her body, Susan was abducted again about a year later. This time her alien captor held a strange baby with thin wispy hair and dark eyes. It held out the baby to Susan, seeming to want her to nurse the child and appearing interested in the reaction that the earthwoman might have to this amazing scenario.

A gynaecologist who experienced an alien encounter was told that the alien race was dying. In another case, from Essex, a spacenapped woman was even told that we are regarded as 'progeny' by the visiting extraterrestrials, who have lost the ability to reproduce for themselves.

If true, then we may literally be alien offspring.

Nobody has found a way to dismiss the spacenapping phenomenon.

Attempts have been made to suggest that witnesses are faking but, as the database grows each year by dozens of new cases from all over the world this seems unlikely.

A bold idea proposes that abductions may be a vision triggered inside the brain when it is being scrambled by high-intensity electrical or microwave radiation – possibly created by a UFO.

Psychologists who have studied dozens of abduction victims have been surprised to find that they are normal people who are by no means prone to fantasy or hallucination. Nor do these cases match the expected patterns found within folk tales. They are so simple and consistent, lacking the wide spread of alien types or motives for visitation that are typical in science fiction.

The consensus is emerging from many stunned researchers that perhaps these very close encounters are all too real.

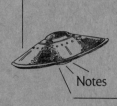
Notes

Perhaps the ultimate proof of the reality of spacenapping involves a New York woman called Linda Napolitano. She was abducted from her high-rise apartment in downtown Manhattan early one night in November 1989. The incident was immediately investigated by UFOlogist Budd Hopkins.

As an alien kidnap has never been witnessed, sceptics often claim that an abduction is just a dream. However, eighteen months after Linda's experience two security guards approached Hopkins and claimed that they were parked outside a Manhattan tower block when they had watched as a woman floated out of her window in the company of strange little beings with large heads and round eyes. She was taken into a hovering UFO which sped off into the waters of the East River.

Further amazing details were to follow. The security guards were driving a world statesman from the United Nations building to the New York heliport when they saw this frightening incident. The politician also saw the abduction take place. Indeed, Hopkins wonders if it was staged for that purpose. If and when this man chooses to reveal the truth the world will never be the same.

But as yet he has remained silent and not been identified.

Further evidence for the validity of abduction cases concerns what are known as 'implants'. Numerous witnesses have claimed that during a spacenapping the aliens have placed a small object inside their bodies – possibly as a monitor device, just as we 'electronically tag' animals in order to follow their migratory behaviour.

Attempts to find these objects using hospital body scans had been unsuccessful. One that was 'sneezed out' by a hapless abductee turned out to be a cotton fibre ball. Another that appeared on a dental x-ray vanished when a second x-ray was taken – the witness insisting that the aliens re-abducted her in the meantime to hijack the evidence.

In August 1995, however, a Californian doctor performed surgery on two spacenap victims and actually extracted three implants from their bodies. These were made of magnetic strips of metal and are still being analysed.

Further surgery during 1996 discovered thirteen more objects in other witnesses and there are researchers now certain that this is the proof we have been waiting for.

As Mulder might insist, the truth is out there: we are pawns in some alien experiment.

Seeking fresh breeding stock from among the human race, the
aliens knew they had found what they wanted when they saw Alf.

Mysteries of the Mind

TELEPATHY

Telepathy is more properly known as 'extra sensory perception' or ESP.

Its name was invented, and its nature first studied, by Dr Joseph B. Rhine in 1927. Along with his wife, Louisa Rhine, he set up a sponsored project at Duke University in North Carolina. For over fifty years they searched for scientific proof that would demonstrate what many who had experienced the phenomenon already knew.

One of their research team, called Zener, invented a pack of 25 playing cards. On these were five sets of symbols (stars, circles, crosses, squares and wavy lines). If one person tried to send the image on a card to someone in another room only telepathy could provide the link.

Because of the nature of Zener cards it was very simple to calculate if the person was merely guessing. Out of 25 cards, five should be guessed correctly. Do the test often enough and you could guarantee no serious deviation from the odds of one in five. If someone succeeded considerably more than that there could be only one explanation. They were using ESP.

Maureen Blyth was eating dinner in one of her favourite restaurants at Liskeard, Cornwall. It was November 1984 and her husband was away on one of his frequent long sea voyages.

Suddenly Maureen found herself staring at the food. It had become inedible. There was no explanation, just a terrible feeling that something had happened to her husband.

Twenty-six hours later Chay Blyth and his travelling companion Eric Blunn were plucked from the freezing waters of the South Atlantic. Their catamaran, in which they were attempting another dangerous crossing, had been overturned by a freak wave and they were left clinging to its hull, hoping for rescue before the cold sea claimed them forever.

There had been seven thousand miles between Mr and Mrs Blyth, but distance had meant nothing that day. Maureen had known instinctively that something was wrong at the very moment that disaster had struck. It was as if Chay's mind had sent out a distress flare and she had picked it up.

This extremely common phenomenon is what researchers call telepathy: the ability of information to be shared between two minds who are not in any other possible contact.

Eventually it was realised that the Zener card experiments and other tests that employed random numbers generated by a computer (much harder to predict) all suffered from one serious flaw.

In real life cases of telepathy there was a bond between the people who shared a message – perhaps they were friends or lovers. There was also an urgency or special requirement, such as danger, that provided the spark. These circumstances were not being reproduced by reading endless symbols off cards and even those gifted at ESP became bored by the task demanded of them.

At the University of Cambridge, Dr Carl Sargent began a new set of experiments in the 1970s using a technique known as the Ganzfeld. The subject was made to relax, their eyes were covered and their hearing blocked by white noise. As a result they 'tuned in' to their inner selves and tried to detect messages through ESP.

The image that someone tried to send to a Ganzfeld subject was deliberately more emotive – such as a painting or a piece of music. Rather than simply guess what it was, the subject was given five paintings or five musical sequences and asked to say which of these was being transmitted.

Ganzfeld experiments have proven very successful. Chance

has been calculated at about one in four, but in some cases accuracy as high as three in four has been produced. Although not all sceptics have been persuaded by this research, it is being duplicated (for example at Stanford University in California) and may yet demonstrate ESP to be a reality.

At Monkey Mia in Western Australia there is a popular tourist attraction. Every day dolphins swim ashore and play with visitors. Wilf Mason, who runs the site, says that the dolphins are incredibly aware of the type of person who comes to play. They 'pick up the vibes', he says, and stay clear if you are not sincere in your intentions.

Dolphins are known to be some of the most intelligent animals in the world. Mammals like ourselves, yet adapted to an aquatic environment, they have a brain capacity akin to our own and a language and social structure that makes them seem eerily human.

It is thought that they might naturally use ESP. So researchers Pat Hayes and Ann Phillips worked with three young dolphins at the University of Miami in Florida. The animals quickly sensed the differences between these two women – one of whom was afraid of water. With her they never left the shallows. Yet they took her expert swimmer colleague for regular rides into deep water.

Eventually the two scientists tried to transmit 'thought pictures' to one dolphin by imagining complex swimming motions. Within days the dolphin was practising what had never been physically demonstrated and had even taught the other two dolphins to do it as well!

Sometimes the ability to read emotions can seem a curse. It was so for *Star Wars* actor Don Henderson.

When filming the TV drama *Bulman* Henderson was called upon to play a scene with his close friend George Pravda. Pravda had the role of a KGB agent who was splitting up from the TV detective. The script called for his return in a future episode, and the actors knew one another socially very well – so this scene would prove difficult. Somehow they would have to pretend that they might never see one another again.

The camera focused on Don Henderson as he wept and said 'goodbye' to his fictional and real life friend. Once in the can the crew came over to congratulate him on such a convincing performance. But Henderson had not been acting. As he had hugged Pravda a chain of information flowed between them. Henderson simply knew that this really was the last time they would be together.

Shortly afterwards George Pravda died of a massive heart attack. He did not even get to see this episode transmitted just a few months later. Somehow – in that emotional bond that acting had summoned up – Don Henderson had sensed an inner truth which crossed the barriers of time and space.

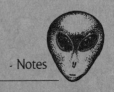
Notes

MIND OVER MATTER

The small town of Rosenheim in Germany is pretty, but quiet. In 1967, however, its small lawyer's office erupted into a fantastic outbreak of what is known as PK (psycho kinesis). Literally translated, this is the ability of a mind to move objects without physical cause – something that physicists since Sir Isaac Newton have considered impossible.

Terrified staff and clients would notice the light bulbs in the corridor sway as if the building was being rocked by an earthquake. The photocopier would go crazy and spew out documents in a demented rage. Colossal phone bills were built up as hundreds of calls were registered to the speaking clock.

In a mild state of panic the lawyers sent for the local ghostbuster, Professor Hans Bender, from the University of Freiburg. However, the effects soon stopped of their own volition, leaving him with just a theory to try to explain what had happened.

In the office was a 19-year-old girl who was bored by her menial work and spent much of the day watching the clock. Professor Bender suggested that she was taking out her emotional frustration by somehow venting a psychic force. But how could this make objects move on their own?

Another kind of mind bender arrived on the scene when Israeli magician Uri Geller became a TV celebrity. Geller's party trick was to hold a spoon or knife and cause it to bend simply by focusing his innate ability to use PK.

The critics soon attacked Geller, insisting he was just using conjuring tricks. Magicians such as America's James 'The Amazing' Randi showed how it could be done through techniques such as sleight of hand, pocketing an already bent spoon and switching it for the unbent one.

Geller went on to confound his critics by taking house keys which could not be substituted and bending these as well. New possible explanations were put forward. But the battle went all the way to the courts, with charge and countercharge about alleged fraud.

Uri certainly had the last laugh. He was never proven to be a fake and was ultimately employed by big business conglomerates to use his abilities to hunt out ore deposits in situations where random drilling would cost billions.

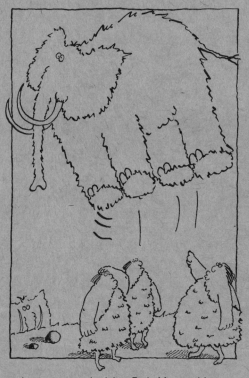

Levitation worked, but Early Man could see
no practical application for it.

PSYCHIC DETECTIVES

Nella Jones was born half Romany and her gypsy heritage has endowed her with powerful psychic visions. She has often used her skills to help the police.

When a painting valued at £2 million was stolen from Kenwood in North London, Nella heard the news whilst doing the ironing. Suddenly images filled her mind which indicated where clues could be found. Within minutes she had sketched a map and had phoned the police directing them where to look.

Next day the police asked her to go with them to the scene of the crime. They had looked where Nella had suggested and found part of the frame of the painting. Could she provide any further clues? Once at Kenwood House the psychic astonished detectives by marching straight into a pond in the grounds. Not hesitating, she waded out and put her hand below the dirty water. Up came a metal object that proved to be the casing from the alarm on the painting. Nella told them to ignore ransom notes that would arrive. The painting would be recovered in a cavernous area that seemed like a cemetery. The nearest cemetery to Kenwood was quickly searched but nothing was found. However, days later the painting was successfully recovered in another cemetery across the city.

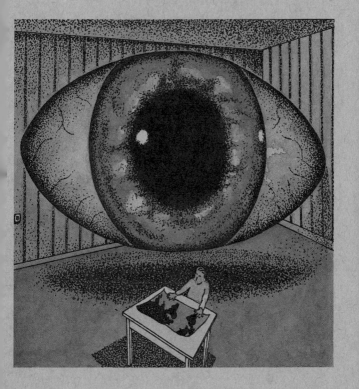

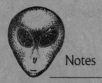

Notes

Young mother Etta Smith from California one day found herself living out a scene from a Hitchcock movie.

In mid-December 1980 pretty nurse Melanie Uribe had vanished as she drove to work in the hills outside Los Angeles. As soon as Etta heard the news on the radio she was swamped by a strange feeling and she just 'knew' what had happened. She saw a vision of the woman lying dead in a canyon.

So upset was Etta by this experience that she drove to the police station and reluctantly told her story to a detective, having pointed out on a map the area where she thought the body lay.

Back home events still preyed on her mind. Would the police take her seriously and investigate? She did not think so. Bundling her two children in to the car she drove to Lopez Canyon and spotted 'rags' on the ground just where she had visualised. Fear now overcame her and she turned around and drove out of there at speed. Flagging down a passing police car she led it back to the scene and there – sure enough – was the body of Melanie Uribe.

DREAMS

The exploration of dreams has an ancient tradition, but science has only just begun to apply its own methods. We have now come to recognise the periods during which we dream as what is called REM sleep. In this state the entire body, apart from the eyes and respiration, is paralysed. The eyes, however, jerk about in rapid motions which characterise the dream state.

Some higher animals, such as cats and dogs, exhibit very rapid eye movements while sleeping. Although we cannot ask them whether they are dreaming scientists think it very possible that they are.

Notes

The mysterious phenomenon of 'déjà vu' may be connected with dreaming. Translated from the French this means 'already seen' and is that eerie sensation most people get from time to time that they are reliving a scene which they have somehow gone through before.

Scientists now believe that, whilst dreams are not normally available to the conscious memory, they might all be stored somewhere in the unconscious mind. Because we dream so much and so frequently there could be literally billions of imagined experiences hidden from our normal recall.

Memory works by the brain matching electrical impulses with certain experiences that we have previously undergone. Once these are matched a familiarity or recognition is registered. The theory is that, if a current experience is closely similar to something from a dream state lurking deep in the subconscious, we may be vaguely aware of that fact but not in any conscious sense. As such, it comes across as a tantalising sense of having seen the events somewhere before – but not in a form that the brain can properly visualise.

In other words, 'déjà vu' does mean we have 'already seen' what is happening to us before. Not in reality – but in a long-forgotten dream.

Notes

The creative power of dreams has long been recognised by artists. Many classic works of literature have begun in this way.

The epic poem 'Kubla Khan' originated in a dream of the poet Coleridge, as did the famous horror story 'Dr Jekyll and Mr Hyde' by Robert Louis Stevenson.

Even scientists have benefited. The chemist Friedrich Kekule was struggling to understand the complex nature of the benzene molecule. He fell asleep with the problem still racing through his head and a dream solved it for him. He saw a mass of snakes coiled around and eating one another's tails. Upon awakening he drew the symbol in a more chemically orientated fashion and immediately had the correct configuration of the benzene molecule.

In cases like this, or that of Alan Turing, who invented the first successful computer in a dream, the subconscious mind had probably already sensed the solution but the waking, conscious mind had not. So in sleep the truth seeped through thanks to the symbolic, punning methods used by the dream self.

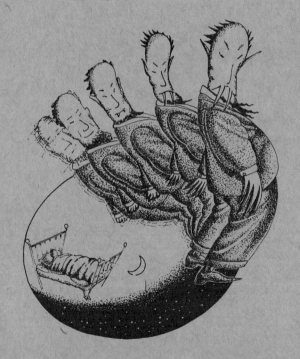

239

MEDIUMS

When the American master magician Harry Houdini died he took one secret with him to the grave. It was a coded message that he hoped to convey from the afterlife to his wife and family.

Houdini had been fascinated by mediums – people who claim to act as a conduit between this world and the next, conveying messages from the deceased to their surviving loved ones. Although he hoped otherwise, he was unconvinced that these people were not playing tricks: either upon themselves through self-delusion, or through outright deception, preying on people when at their most vulnerable.

Using testing methods and tricks at their seances, the magician gave dozens of mediums the chance to prove themselves. Try as he might Houdini never found one he considered to be genuine. This is why he took the coded message with him, arguing that if there is anyone out there who can contact the dead he would find them from the afterlife and get in touch.

After sixty years the world is still waiting to hear from Harry Houdini.

The most popular method of trying to get in touch with the 'other side' is the ouija board – derived from the French and German words for 'yes'. Yes, of course, is the answer that mediums seek when they use the lettered board and pointer to ask into the ether: is there anybody there?

A board game version of 'ouija' was introduced into Europe and America in 1969 but soon came under fire from both Christian movements and psychologists. They argued that it was sacreligious and also potentially hazardous to a person's mental health should they take seriously what sceptics believe to be just the ramblings of the subconscious mind.

Surprisingly, even mediums are hostile to the ouija board, contrary to impression given by movie dramas. They confirm that it is possible for spirits to take control of a person's hands and move the ouija to spell out words and sentences. Unfortunately the spirits most readily able to communicate in this way are on what mediums call the 'lower astral planes'. These are unfriendly souls clinging to the earth and, perhaps resentful of their lost corporeal existence, may have evil intent. Consequently the unwary user of a ouija board could find themselves in psychic deep water.

Actor Michael Bentine was a medium and had long known that he could 'tune in' to the other side. He believed it is a natural gift that many of us share.

During a gruelling tour in 1979 he received several messages of impending doom. The words 'blood sacrifice' kept booming in his head. The truth was revealed by a call from the police with the tragic news that Bentine's friend, MP Airey Neave, had just been killed by a massive IRA car bomb. Bentine had served with Neave in the intelligence service and was currently working with the politician on new air safety regulations. The police had called in case he was also a target, given his association with the victim. As Michael absorbed the shock news he suddenly felt uplifted and almost seemed to experience a connection with his dead friend. The words 'And all the trumpets sounded for him on the other side' entered Bentine's head. Days later Michael sat in the church of St Martins-in-the-Fields attending the memorial service for Airey Neave. Prime Minister Margaret Thatcher spoke the eulogy using exactly the same words that Bentine had heard. Whilst Michael Bentine did not fully understand how or why these things happened to him he had no doubt of one thing: 'We do not die; we are composed of energy. You cannot destroy energy. It's a scientific fact.'

Notes

At the Stanford Research Institute in Menlo Park, California they work regularly with people who go out of their minds. Scientists Drs Targ and Puthoff investigate cases of 'out of the body' experiences – or OOBEs – in which people say that they float out of themselves and view the world from a disembodied state. They then receive messages, rather like mediums do.

Many people experience an OOBE as a one-off event, possibly during sleep or deep relaxation. Indeed, 'flying dreams,' which are extremely common, may be the same thing.

However, Targ and Puthoff are more concerned with rare subjects who can take their minds out of their bodies almost at will. One such man is called Blue Harary. He demonstrated his abilities by experiments which the scientists call 'remote viewing'.

In these tests one of the research staff would go to a location randomly selected by computer and subjects like Harary would try to float free and find them, in a sort of psychic version of hide and seek. Later they would describe the venue and try to pick out the correct site from the computer list. Some extraordinary results have been achieved.

So successful has been research into OOBEs that Stanford has been contacted by the US intelligence agency, the CIA. Working with some of their top psychics the aptly named 'spooks' at the agency wanted to see if OOBEs could prove effective in spy missions.

Several successful 'out of body' trippers were given map coordinates and asked to describe what they could see at this spot simply by entering an OOBE. They did so and came up with various accounts of an island and the buildings located there.

The target was a top secret Soviet base complete with missile silos. It was remote and well hidden, proving very difficult to film even with the highly sophisticated surveillance satellites then in orbit. The psychics quickly demonstrated their worth, producing better evidence than the multi-billion dollar space hardware could achieve – just by going out of their minds.

As a result many nations now have 'psychic research programmes' under the control of their intelligences services. There have even been experiments in remote viewing of Soviet cosmonauts in earth orbit.

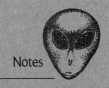

Notes

Notes

New Yorker Bill Tenuto is one of the most remarkable of his breed. Known as a 'direct voice medium' he claims not simply to hear voices or receive messages from the other side but to allow the deceased to speak through him.

His most famous contact is with the murdered singer and ex-Beatle John Lennon. Speaking through Tenuto (and changing his normal accent to a Liverpudlian drawl) Lennon has conveyed hours of messages about his continued existence.

Lennon claims to have forgiven the man who shot him outside his Central Park apartment in 1980. He also says that a major transformation is overcoming the world. Speaking in 1983 he predicted that there would be a wide belief in the paranormal sweeping the planet and a massive rise in spiritual values. A bloodless revolution would overthrow evil.

All of these have since occurred – from the fall of Communism to the dramatic rise in public awareness of the supernatural, exemplified by TV series like *The X-Files* and *Strange but True?*

Lennon more enigmatically says that he works with an organisation called the White Brotherhood. These discarnate entities are trying to convey spiritual messages to earth and help us in our progress. Other members of this cosmic cavalry include, improbably, John Wayne and Elvis Presley!

LIFE AFTER DEATH

When someone dies what happens to them? Do they simply disappear into oblivion, or does some part of them live on in another dimension?

Frank Musgrove studied blind people as a professional researcher and describes a remarkable case in which a man, blind for 21 years, suffered a stroke and entered a deep coma. In this state for many weeks, he seemed virtually dead to the world and visitors who came to the hospital were unable to communicate. This included one relative who had been out of touch for years and had brought along her son, whom the man had never met.

When the patient recovered from his ordeal he described an astonishing experience. Whilst in the coma he had gone to 'another world' in which he could see again. In this place he had been able to look down from above and watch visitors come and go.

The woman and her son had been seen and were described by this man, even though this was not medically possible. After recovery from his stroke, of course, the patient was still blind. But somehow in that other dimension visited during his coma such physical impediments had meant nothing.

Notes

There are now hundreds of cases of what are known as 'near death experiences', in which a person comes very close to death during an accident or surgery. According to all logic they should experience nothing. But this is not the case. Very often they have profound visions of another world.

A five-year-old boy in a hospital in the north of England told of how he 'awoke' during the middle of emergency heart surgery to watch the whole procedure while floating in mid-air. There was no pain. He felt happy and relaxed. He watched surgeons insert a plastic valve into his heart and amazed doctors later by describing this in detail.

But all he was really concerned about was the question he asked his mother. 'Mummy – why wouldn't the doctors talk to me when I was floating up by the ceiling?'

The worst possible nightmare befell an American GI during the Vietnam War. He stood on a landmine and was hit by a rocket almost simultaneously. The shock propelled him out of his body.

Looking on in an oddly calm manner, the soldier watched as his broken body was looted and zipped into a bag. As far as his comrades were concerned he was dead. Yet he knew that he was still alive, watching the scene unfold as if it were a horror film on TV.

During the next hour or two time lost all meaning as the GI floated in another world, seeing bright lights and sensing that he could leave at any time. But something pulled him back towards earth. He clung desperately to life.

Suddenly the soldier re-entered his body and his muscles jerked. He was just in time. The terrified mortician, eyes wide open in shock, was so certain that the GI was dead that he was just about to inject embalming fluid into his veins.

Now that's what I call a near death experience.

So what is life like in heaven? There are plenty of stories from those who have been there and come back.

According to most versions it is very like a duplicate of earth. Indeed, many who die do not realise at first that they are dead because of these similarities. Yet everything there is controlled by thought. What you imagine is what appears. The afterlife is like a great big thought.

Not that the tales are without anomalies.

One man told his wife that she had no need to worry. There are plenty of supermarkets on the other side, so she could still do her weekly shopping.

Baseball star Babe Ruth is still in the game, it seems, part of a league of deceased All Stars.

And Hollywood legends Bud Abbott and Lou Costello have reported to visitors that they have made 64 new movies since their demise but are desperate for their ventures to be seen on earth as well as in the afterlife. All that any enterprising director needs is a camera that can film life in heaven.

Anybody who comes up with one would surely get a nomination for an Oscar!

Published by MQ Publications Ltd
254-258 Goswell Road, London EC1V 7EB

Copyright © MQ Publications Ltd 1997

Text © Jenny Randalls 1997
Illustrations © Philip Norman 1997

ISBN: 1-897954-11-5

Printed and bound in China